Freedom From Stress

J.P. Vaswani

Compiled and Edited by
Dr. Prabha Sampath
and
Krishna Kumari

New Dawn

NEW DAWN
An imprint of Sterling Publishers (P) Ltd.
A-59 Okhla Industrial Area, Phase-II,
New Delhi-110020.
Tel: 26387070, 26386209, Fax: 91-11-26383788
E-mail: ghai@nde.vsnl.net.in www.sterlingpublishers.com

The Little Book Of Freedom From Stress
©2003, Sterling Publishers Private Limited
ISBN 81 207 2580 8

All rights are reserved. No part of this publication may be reproduced, stored in a retrieval system or transmitted, in any form or by any means, mechanical, photocopying, recording or otherwise, without prior written permission of the publisher.

Published by Sterling Publishers Pvt. Ltd., New Delhi-110020.
Lasertypeset by Vikas Compographics, New Delhi-110020.
Printed at Sai Early Learners Pvt. Ltd., New Delhi-110020.

Contents

Stress	5
The Causes Of Stress	10
Adopt A Positive Attitude To Life	21
Do Not Anticipate Trouble	28
Live In The Present!	32
Do Not Hold A Grudge Against Anyone In The Heart Within You	39
Cultivate The Spirit Of Gratitude	41
Simplify Your Life!	44
Develop A Healthy Sense Of Humour	50
Develop Faith, Cultivate Faith	57
Take Care Of Your Breathing	64
You Must Practise The Technique Of Relaxation	66

Practise Silence Everyday	76
Help Others	80
Stress Busters	85

Stress

I was in Mumbai when a man met me and asked me: "What do you think of Mumbai?"

"It is a good place, if only you know how to live in the right way," I said to him.

"I feel Mumbai is awful," he exclaimed. "The very air is full of stress and tension."

I looked upwards for a minute and then said to him: "My brother, it is true the air of Mumbai is full of pollution; but there is no tension or stress in the air. Stress is not in the air but it is in the minds of the people who breathe the air. You can be master of stress or you can let stress master you."

The world today is full of tension. Wherever I go, I find people are tense and nervous. Stress and tension are more common in their incidence than the common cold.

Today hospitals are full of patients who suffer from diseases due to stress. Stress is the cause of a number of physical ailments. Stress keeps on accumulating in the minds of the people until, one day, it manifests itself in the form of one ailment or the other.

Several years ago, a book was published, entitled *Cosmic Factors in Disease*. It was written by an eminent physician, Dr. Guirdham. In the book he tells us that tension and stress cause a number of diseases including hypertension, heart attack, nervous break down, malfunctioning of the colon, pain in the back of the neck, asthma, constipation, duodenal ulcers, migraine and certain forms of epilepsy. Stress and tension also cause insomnia – sleeplessness. So it is, that the demand for sleeping pills keeps on growing in our cities.

Sleep is a natural restorative process. After a day's hard work, man should be able to sleep peacefully; but today, many, alas, have lost the gift of sound sleep. There was a time, whenever

I spoke, I would find some people in the audience had gone off to sleep. But today, it is difficult to put people to sleep thus – for they are so tensed and highly-strung.

The statistics are frightening, whenever we consider them. The Americans are very systematic and they have statistics for all these matters. We can take America as a sample for the rest of the world. What does the picture look like there? We are told that:

- One million Americans have a heart attack each year
- 13 million doses of tranquilizers and sedatives are prescribed yearly
- 8 million Americans are said to have stomach ulcers
- There are an estimated 50,000 stress-related suicides every year
- There are 12 million alcoholics in the US

Some doctors actually believe that nearly 80% of the illnesses treated in the US are emotionally induced illnesses (EII).

What is this "Stress" that we are talking about? It is a much-used, much misused term. Dr. Hars Seyle, expert on stress-management, tells us: "Stress is the wear and tear on your body caused by life's events." It is the sum total of the body's physical, mental, and chemical reactions to circumstances which cause fear, irritation, worry, anxiety and excitement.

There are hundreds of experiences in our everyday life which cause stress. These stress – causing events are called *stressors*. These *stressors* can create good stress (positive stress) or *distress* (negative stress). Normally, our body and its systems are conditioned to cope with stressors. But there is an optimum level at which each one of us can cope with stress and still function well. When the limit is exceeded, we become victims of stress.

Too little stress makes life dull, boring, irritable and apathetic. Too much stress overwhelms a person, leading to many of the ailments mentioned earlier.

Stress originates from a French word which means constriction or delimitation. True it is that stressful situations seem to squeeze us, limit our emotions and reactions. Stress therefore, is regarded as a potential killer. It saps one's energy and undermines one's well-being.

Stress is purely subjective. What is a stressful situation for one person, may be child's play for another. For instance, if a person is asked to say a few words to a large gathering, he may panic and lose his nerve completely. A fluent public speaker, on the other hand, would regard it as an opportunity, and end up speaking for a long time!

The Causes Of Stress

Man's way of life in the modern age is one of the main causes of stress. Somehow modern life and stress seem to go together. The way we live, the way we work, the way we talk, the way we function everyday, contribute to the building up of stress. People rush about all the time, as though they were carrying the entire burden of the world upon their shoulders. People rush about, accumulating what they think they need – only to realize that they don't need it at all. They resemble squirrels in a cage - running, running all the time - but getting nowhere.

We seem to be in a hurry all the time! It is not only when we are on our feet that we are hurrying; when we are seated, at rest, our minds are rushing somewhere or the other. We may be waiting in an outer office, waiting for an appointment with a doctor, waiting for an interview call – but we are hurrying, rushing in our thoughts. This mental rush, this mental hurry is one of the main causes of tension.

We need to take it easy! Take it easy my brother! Take it easy, sister! There is a word which Spanish people use often. Whenever two Spaniards meet, they say to each other, "Tranquilo! Tranquilo!" Tranquilo means – take it easy! This is the message which all of us need today – Take it easy! Take it easy!

A white man once saw a black man sitting underneath a tree. The white man disapproved of the black man, for he felt that he was wasting time.

"What are you doing Tom?" the white man asked him sternly.

"Why sir, I'm just enjoying myself," Tom replied.

"Why don't you get up and work, Tom?" the white man said to him in a tone of disapproval.

"What for?" Tom wanted to know.

"If you work hard, you will be able to earn money!" explained the white man patiently.

"But what for sir?" Tom persisted.

"If you make money, you can save some of it."

"What for?"

"If you save money, you can have plenty of leisure."

"What for?"

"If you have leisure you can go out on a holiday."

"What for?"

"If you go out on a holiday you will be able to enjoy life."

"But sir," exclaimed Tom, "that's what I'm doing already!"

We don't have to be lazy like the man in the story – but atleast, we must avoid needless hurry. As the proverb tells us, "Haste makes waste". And a lesser known Spanish saying warns us:

"He who pours water hastily into a bottle spills more than goes in."

Thomas Fuller says that haste and rashness are like storms and tempests which break and wreck people's lives and their businesses. The great athletic trainer, William Muldoon observed: "People don't die of disease; they die of internal combustion." Internal combustion! As we rush about our life, stress keeps on building in the mind within, until it leads us to a nervous breakdown or a heart attack.

Car drivers are so rash today. All drivers seem to be in a dreadful hurry to get somewhere - for the seed of rashness is in all of us. Traffic signals are meant to control this rashness and allow people to drive safely, smoothly across intersections. Alas, many of us have forgotten what signals are meant for. The Red says Stop; the Green says Go; and Amber tells us to Wait.

They asked a little boy if he knew what the lights in the traffic signals stood for. "Sure," he replied.

"I've seen my daddy drive past so many signals. Red means stop; green means go and amber means go fast!"

When we come across a red signal, we can switch off the engine, relax and wait for a couple of minutes. But what we do is fret and fume; we grow impatient; we honk loudly, disturbing the motorists around us, annoying everyone and giving vent to our temper!

Charles Swindoll once found himself with several pressing commitments within a short span of time. He became tense and panic-stricken. He was snapping at his wife; gobbling his food at mealtime.

"These were classic symptoms of irritation," he recalled. "Before long, it all began to recoil upon me. The peace of my home was lost completely."

One evening at dinner, he found that his little daughter was trying to tell him something. Earnest and anxious, she came up to him and said, "Papa! Something exciting happened at school today. Can I say it to you very quickly?"

Something awoke in Swindoll. He hugged his little girl and said to her, "Tell Papa everything honey! And you don't have to hurry. Tell me slowly."

"I'll tell you slowly Papa," said the child. "But are you sure you can listen slowly?"

How much do we lose out on the little joys of life when we cannot walk, talk, think or *listen* slowly!

Another cause of stress is irritation. We give in again and again to irritation. We may not always show it – but the irritation inside burns up our emotional energy uselessly. Everytime you are irritated, you are burning up valuable emotional energy, which can be used constructively.

We must develop the patience to curb irritation. A Dutch proverb tells us: "A handful of patience is worth more than a bushel of brains." Wise men like Benjamin Franklin would agree: "He that can have patience can have what he will."

Mahatma Gandhi met with so many obstacles, very many, trying situations and a thousand frustrating delays during the course of the struggle for India's Independence. But he learnt to conquer his impatience and irritation. He once remarked: "I have learnt through bitter experience the one supreme lesson – to conserve my impatience. As heat conserved is transmitted into energy, even so, anger controlled can move the world."

A sister once said to me, "Everytime my neighbour's cat gets into my garden, I get irritated." Another lady often says, "The very sight of my sister-in-law irritates me." And there is a brother who says, "The moment I see my partner, something gets into me."

What insignificant events cause irritation to us! A cat, a friend, a relative – and what not! If we cannot change the people around us, we can at least try to change our reactions to them!

Yet another cause of stress is that we are overwhelmed by the problems we face. I always say that problems are wonderful presents that are thrown at us by Providence – only, we fail to recognise the gift because it comes wrapped up in a soiled package. The word 'problem' is derived from the Latin word "pro balo" and means that which is deliberately thrown in our way. It is because we react to problems negatively that we create panic and stress within us.

It has been said that a problem is like a pebble. If you hold it close to your eye, it seems magnified, and it blocks your entire vision. If you hold it at arm's length, you can see its shape, its colour and its size. If you drop it at your feet, you can effortlessly walk over it!

Another reason why we react negatively to stress situations is mental fatigue and exhaustion. We are often apt to underestimate the demands of intellectual or mental work, as against hard, physical labour. Psychiatrists say that people who work with their brains need more sleep and rest than manual workers. When mental fatigue sets in, we cannot think clearly or react reasonably.

Picture to yourself a man sitting slouched on a sofa. His shoulders are drooping. His head is down, and he is holding his chin in both his hands. His entire body seems to be drooping.

Is not this the condition of many of us at the end of a day's work? What a weary burden we have made of a day – which had been God's brand new gift to us just a few hours ago?

A man went to his Guru, complaining of utter fatigue and exhaustion. "Swamiji, I just cannot cope any more," he complained. "Please help me!"

The Guru took him to an inner chamber, where there were two clocks on the table. Both were ticking away merrily. One was a freestanding clock; the other was connected to the mains with a power cable.

"This clock will keep going for less than 24 hours," said the Guru, pointing to the first one. "After just one day, it will slow down and begin to lose time gradually. I have to come in every morning and wind it up to keep it going, or else it will soon come to a stop."

He pointed to the electric clock. "This one you can see, is connected to a source of high power, and with the energy from that source, it keeps going, on and on. It does not need to be wound up every day. It just goes on, ticking merrily."

The man stared at the two clocks, unable to understand what the Guru was saying.

"You must connect yourself to God – the Source of the highest, purest and best energy in the Universe," said the Guru. " Then you will not have to be pushed from outside. No one will have to wind you, or give you a boost. You will draw all the energy and wisdom of the Universe through your connection with God, and nothing can stop you!"

The world looks bleak and miserable to those who are fatigued. Give the body enough sleep; recharge your heart and soul by connecting yourself to God constantly. Then, your soul can work to relieve your stress and restore your depleted energy.

Practical Suggestions:
Practical Suggestion No. 1
Adopt A Positive Attitude To Life

This cannot be done in a day. But you must begin now! Never put off for tomorrow, what you can do today. Never put off for later, what you can do right away.

Many people say, "I'll change my attitude one of these days." One of these days is none of these days! Affirm to yourself: "Right now, from this moment, I shall adopt a positive attitude." All the great ones of humanity have borne testimony to the great truth that man is his own friend; and man is his own foe. In the measure in which we think good thoughts, positive thoughts, we become our own friends. In the measure we think negative thoughts, thoughts of defeat and despair, we turn into our own enemies.

No one outside of us can harm us. It is only we who harm ourselves. It is very easy to lay the blame at the door of another. It is so easy to say, "It's only because of A or B that I am in trouble now." But the truth is, no one outside of us has this power. Someone has said, "The longer I live, the more convinced I become, that life is 10% what happens to us and 90% how we respond to it." Truly has it been said, "Attitude is more important than education, bank balance, influence, position and power and the circumstances in which we are placed. If we change our attitude, we can change our lives."

When attitudes are right, there is no barrier we cannot cross, no dream we cannot realize, no goals we cannot achieve, no challenges we cannot overcome. It was John Miller who said, "Your living is determined not so much by what life brings to you, as by the attitude you bring to life."

Dr. Radhakrishnan made his first visit to the United States when John F. Kennedy was the President. The weather was dark and stormy in Washington; and when Dr. Radhakrishnan alighted from the plane, it began to pour cats and dogs, as the expression goes.

The young American President greeted his Indian counterpart with a warm handshake and a smile. "I'm so sorry we have such bad weather during your visit," he remarked courteously.

The philosopher-statesman smiled. "We can't change bad things, Mr. President," he observed. "But we can change our attitude to them."

A few years ago I was in Delhi, when I was invited by Doordarshan to visit their studios. There I met a wonderful man. He had lost both his arms in an accident. But he had a positive attitude. He trained his feet so that he could take up the job of composing in a press. With a smile on his face and a feeling of joy, he said, "I earn Rs. 500 a month. I am not a burden on anyone."

There was another man whom I met in Pune. He was sitting by the wayside, and he had neither feet nor legs.

"What happened to you?" I asked him.

"Nothing!" he replied. "I was born this way."

"May I ask, who takes care of you, my friend?"

"My mother - and above all, God."

"Do you find it difficult, inconvenient to move about?"

"Do you find it difficult and inconvenient that you don't have wings?" he asked me. "Don't you think it would be far better if you could fly on your own, rather than wait to catch a plane?"

"Life is a matter of habit," he added. "If you start complaining, there is so much to complain about. It is the attitude that counts."

The following steps will help us to cultivate a positive attitude:

- Empty your mind of all negative thoughts and fill it with fresh, invigorating, positive thoughts. Set aside time everyday, to give your mind a good shampoo.

- An expert tailor says that the best way to keep clothes in good shape is to make sure that the pockets are emptied when they are hung up. We may infer from this, that the best way to keep ourselves and our lives in good shape is to empty our minds of all worries, anxieties, tensions and negative thoughts before we retire for the night. We can then begin the new day with energy, vigour and freshness.

- Whenever your mind is driving you towards negative thinking, affirm to yourself positive thoughts that will change the track of your thinking.

- The world's scriptures are full of dynamic, positive, energetic thoughts which have the power to boost your morale and keep your spirits high. Choose any thought that appeals to you and repeat it to yourself constantly.

The great psychiatrist, Karl Menninger, has said: "Think big. Men do not break down because they are defeated, but only because they think they are." Do not think defeat; think victory. Think big, act big; believe big; pray big. This is the formula to overcome stress.

A world famous shoe manufacturer took a decision to expand his business, by setting up a new branch in a remote, little-known country. He called up one of his marketing managers and asked him to take the next flight to the country and explore the possibility of setting up a new factory there.

The young executive flew out the very next day. But within 24 hours of reaching there he called up his boss. "This place is no good for our business," he said gloomily. "People do not wear shoes out here. We had better forget any notion of setting up a factory here. It simply won't do. And I am catching the next flight home."

The boss was highly dissatisfied with the report. He had set his heart on doing what he wanted. So he called up another young manager and sent him out with the same order.

Within a few hours of landing there, the young man called up in great excitement. "This place is unbelievable," he exclaimed. "Our business is going to boom out here. These people don't even know what shoes are like. When we introduce shoes here, we shall have a whole, new, untapped market. Send in our planners and designers as soon as you can. We must set up a factory here and we shall win all the way!"

What a difference a positive attitude can make!

Practical Suggestion No. 2
Do Not Anticipate Trouble

There are so many who are given to this habit of anticipating troubles. They do it most of the time – and in the process they lose much of the joy of living. "O what will happen to me?" "What will be my condition if this were to happen?" and so on.

There are old men who are afraid to go out for a walk. "If I go out, I may slip and break a bone," they say, denying themselves one of the simple pleasures of life. There are men who will refuse to fly anywhere. I asked one of them the reason, and he said, "My father died in an air crash." Supposing you were to ask this man, "How did your mother die?" He is likely to reply, "She died peacefully, in bed"! Can this man avoid sleeping in his bed at night?

There was a woman whose daughter was late in returning home one night. The mother imagined that all sorts of misfortunes had befallen the child. Within 15 minutes, she began calling up the city hospitals to find out if a girl had been admitted that evening. She was about to ring the police station to file a complaint, when the girl walked into the house, happily, humming a tune. The mother was reduced to the state of a nervous wreck.

It was Jesus who said: "Sufficient unto the day is the evil thereof." We have all been endowed with sufficient strength. God has blessed us with the means and resources to tackle our life each day. God does not dwell in the Heavens above, He is here in the heart within you. He gives you the strength to face the troubles that you may have to face on any given day.

Anticipating troubles leads to unnecessary worry. We are told that worry is derived from two different Anglo Saxon roots which mean, "harm" and "wolf". True, worry is harmful – and it bites and tears us even as a wolf mauls a lamb. A little worry or anxiety can be helpful, for it keeps us on the alert, and prepares us for action. But excessive worry has the opposite effect – it paralyses the will and makes us unfit for action. It clouds our vision and distracts the thinking process.

An old story tells us of an angel who met a man carrying a heavy sack on his back.

"What is it that you carry on your back, my friend?" enquired the angel.

"My worries," sighed the man. "Truly, they are a terrible burden."

"Put down the sack," said the angel, "and let me see your worries."

When the sack was opened, it was empty!

The man was astonished. He had two great worries: one was about yesterday, which he now saw was past; the other of tomorrow, which had not yet arrived!

The angel told him, "You have no worries. Throw the sack away."

And so it is that we have the wise saying, "In trouble to be troubled is to have your troubles doubled."

Practical Suggestion No. 3
Live In The Present!

Whenever we are confronted by a problem or a stressful situation, we tend to look all over it, all around it, with all its complexities and demands, all at once. Then we are overwhelmed. We begin to panic. Our hearts beat faster. Our breathing becomes quick and shallow. Our blood pressure rises. We become tense. We feel knots in our stomach. All these are symptoms of acute stress.

It is at a time like this that we should think in terms of day-tight compartments. What do I mean by day-tight compartments? We have all heard of water-tight compartments: you fill a vessel with water to the brim, until it can hold no more. If any more water is poured in, it will spill out. A tight lid is put on the container. No more water can go into it. The water inside cannot spill out either.

Likewise, organize your life in day-tight compartments. Draw a circle to represent a 24-hour period. Into this circle put in all the work and effort that you think you can achieve conveniently, comfortably, during those 24 hours. Forget everything else. True, there is a lot of work that remains to be done – but don't bother about it. This is all the work you can do in 24 hours. Put a cap over it. After it is done, think and plan for the next 24 hours.

Sometimes the pressure is so high, that even the 24-hour compartment may seem too big. Then you can think in terms of six-hour compartments or even one-hour compartments. Draw a circle to represent a one-hour compartment. Pour into it all the work you can comfortably do in the next one hour. Don't think of the work that remains to be done – it can wait. All your attention must be focussed on the work that you can do during the next one hour. But one thing you must do – you must see that you finish the work you have assigned yourself before you move to the next compartment. You will then have the pleasure and satisfaction of having achieved what you set out to do. And this is no small matter!

I tell people again and again: you should not make yourself miserable by thinking of the past or of the future. The past is a cancelled cheque. The future is a promissory note. The present is the only cash in hand. Use it wisely and well. Make the most of it!

When you work in this way, organizing your life in day-tight, or six-hour or one-hour compartments, you will find that you have hit upon a powerful and effective way of overcoming stress. This is what we call living in the present. If we wish to overcome stress, we must live in the present. You will see how happy, healthy, relaxed you can be, if you live in the present.

They asked a woman-saint, "How did you arrive at the lofty heights you have reached? What was the *tapasya* you performed to attain such a state?

We always find you smiling and cheerful. Pray, tell us what is the secret of this happy state!"

The saint replied, "My secret is a very simple one. When I eat, I eat. When I work, I work. When I sleep, I sleep."

The people were puzzled. They said to her, "But that is what we do, too! We eat when we eat; we work when we work, and we sleep when we sleep."

"No," she said. "When you eat, your mind travels far. You think of so many things that you are not even aware of the food you are eating. You don't enjoy the food. You should taste every morsel, chew it, swallow it. Alas, you don't do this! And when you work, you are thinking of a thousand things. You must live in the present!"

Therefore, do only one thing at a time. Doing more than one thing at a time divides your attention, increases your stress. When you are talking to someone, give him your full attention. It may be just a little matter – but it saves you from considerable stress. Give your best to what you are doing. Let all your energy and attention be focussed on the task at hand. When the mind is one pointed it is capable of concentration and is free from tension.

Practical Suggestion No. 4

Do Not Hold A Grudge Against Anyone In The Heart Within You

When you hold a grudge against someone, it only disturbs your peace of mind. Hatred is self-punishment. Very often, our ill-will and resentment cannot touch the other person – but we are poisoned by our negative feelings. We lose our inner peace and this leads to stress.

Has someone wronged you? Has someone cheated you? Has someone maligned you? Has someone taken undue advantage of you? Has someone spread scandals against you? Then forgive them, before forgiveness is asked.

We need to grow in the spirit of forgiveness if we wish to conquer stress. And your forgiveness must be total and complete. I tell my friends: every night as you retire, think of all the people who have wronged you or harmed you during the day; and actually call out their names: Mr. A, I forgive you. Mrs. B, I forgive you. Miss. C, I forgive you. You will find that you can sleep soundly! And you are sure to have pleasant and beautiful dreams.

The spirit of forgiveness is lacking in our lives today. And therefore, our stress keeps on growing from more to more. It keeps on mounting, until it breaks out in the form of some physical ailment or the other.

A learned Professor of great academic repute was engaging his class at the University. Having delivered an introduction, he pointed to one of the students and asked him to read aloud from the text.

The student arose and began to read, holding his book in his left hand. "That's not the way to behave in class," said the Professor sharply. "Take your book in your right hand and be seated."

The student stopped short. After a moment or two, he silently held up his right arm – he did not have a right hand!

The class grew strangely silent. Everyone felt uncomfortable and pained.

The Professor sat still, dumb-founded. Then he rose from his seat and walked slowly down to where the young man stood. He put his arm around him and said with tears in his eyes, "I am truly sorry. I have spoken in haste. Will you please forgive me?"

Forgiveness is the precious lubricant which keeps all our relationships smooth and friction-free. We often find doors and windows and gates beginning to groan and squeak when they have not been oiled. Even so do we begin to squeak under stress – forgiveness can take the squeaks away!

A young mother brought her two quarrelling children together and insisted that they made up with each other. "Say sorry to your brother," she said to her daughter. "And you – say sorry to your sister!"

"Sorry!" snapped the girl. "I am saying sorry from the outside because mummy asked me to. But inside I am still very angry with you!"

This is not the spirit of true forgiveness. It does not lie in words or phrases. It must come from the heart within.

And last, but not the least, learn to forgive yourself. Self-reproach and guilt only waste your spiritual energy. Forgive yourself – and live for today.

Practical Suggestion No. 5
Cultivate The Spirit Of Gratitude

There are a thousand blessings that God has bestowed upon us. We are rarely conscious of these – we only complain about what we lack. This adds to the stress and tension of our lives.

So many of us say, "I don't know why God is doing this to me. I don't deserve it." How many of us ever say, "Such a wonderful thing happened to me today. I don't know how it came to pass – for I don't deserve it"?

Whenever people come to me in a state of tension and depression, I tell them to count their blessings. Not just count them in the mind – but actually write them down and make a list of them. When you actually start making a list, you will surely find that you have a lot to be grateful for!

It is hard to feel stressed or tense, when your heart overflows with gratitude!

There is a fruit found in Africa, called the tasteberry. It is said that when you have eaten the berry, all else that you eat subsequently becomes sweet or pleasant to taste. Even sour or bitter food tastes good – such is the extraordinary effect of the tasteberry!

Gratitude is the tasteberry of the soul. Savour it, and you will not be subject to stress and tension.

A group of pilgrims were on their way to a remote shrine in the mountains. The journey was a long and hazardous one. The narrow path was steep and slippery, and progress was slow. The weather was freezing, and food and water had to be carefully rationed. As the days passed, a feeling of gloom and pessimism descended over the group.

It was decided that, at the next night's stop, a meeting would be held to discuss their problems.

When the pilgrims gathered around the campfire that night, one of them began to speak. "Before we speak of anything else, let us thank the Lord for His grace and kindness. We have come thus far with no loss of life – and all of us are still on our feet."

Absolute silence followed the simple words of gratitude. No one had any complaints to make. Everyone felt that they were really fortunate to have come thus far.

Such is the change, the transformation that gratitude can bring about! A thankful heart enables us to look at the brighter side of life – and get the right perspective.

Practical Suggestion No. 6
Simplify Your Life!

"The world is too much with us," wrote the poet Wordsworth. Truer words were never spoken! Caught in the mad rush for possessions, power and material acquisitions, we become prime targets for stress.

I happened to look around me when the car I was travelling in, was caught in a traffic jam on a busy road in Mumbai. All around us were glorious, impressive and very expensive automobiles. Music was blaring aloud from a few of them. Impatient drivers and passengers were reacting with anger and irritation. Agitated men were talking urgently through their cell phones.

How many are the gadgets that modern technology has blessed us with – and they do not seem to make us happy! They only add to the stress and tension of our lives!

Some people are always talking into three telephones at one time – while a cell phone sings aloud from their shirt-pocket.

I have seen young men and women walk down parks and green lanes with ear-phones from their stereos around their heads – lost to the world of beauty around them.

Some people are so lost in the rush for material possessions. Driven by desire, ambition and the will to amass more and more, they run race after race – until they forget what they wanted in the first place. They are so driven by the need to succeed that they fill their life with stress.

It was a wise man who said: it is only the simple things of life that endure; it is the fundamentals of life that matter – not the artificialities.

Keep it simple! That is the *mantra* which can help you reduce stress and tension. Keep it simple! Possessions and acquisitions may seem marvellous – but after a while, you do not own them – they own you.

A Tao story tells us of an artist who was so gifted that his fame spread all over the land. One day, he painted the picture of a snake. It was so lifelike, so real that viewers seemed to hear it hiss!

They praised the picture to the skies. The artist was so carried away by his own success and the adulation of his fans that he started painting the picture again. He touched up the snake; he made its eyes glow; he outlined the fangs so that they seemed to dart at you! He could not stop; he went on and painted feet on the snake!

The expression, "Painting feet on a snake," has become a Chinese saying – an aphorism. It refers to situations that are needlessly made more complicated by people who do not know when and where to stop.

When our life becomes complicated with power and possessions, we move further and further away from the simple joys and pleasures of life. We fail to notice the green grass and the fresh morning flowers. We don't have time to hear birds singing or watch our little ones smiling. We drift away from the state of childlike innocence and simple joy – which is our basic nature.

Simplicity is not self-denial. It is a return to those values that matter most in life. It emphasizes spontaneity and intuition. It helps us to rediscover the feeling of wonder and joy that we have lost as adults.

There are men who remain untouched, untainted by possessions – though that is rare! There was a wealthy businessman, who was also a sincere, simple soul. He owned an expensive jet in which he flew about from place to place. They asked him if he enjoyed his private plane. His reply was significant. He said it was certainly very convenient; but he had managed to travel without his own plane earlier; in fact, when he had been young – and poor – he could not have dreamt of owning a jet – but it did not stop him from being happy.

A wealthy and famous actress was being interviewed on television. She had made a fortune that year – over a billion dollars. "Does it make you feel good?" she was asked.

"Yes and no," she replied thoughtfully. "Everyone thinks it's marvellous. So many people flock around me. But I really do not know who are my true friends and who are with me only for the money and the glamour. As for my daily life – it has not changed much, except that I work harder now."

A group of young men and women were walking across a shopping mall. They were happy and relaxed; they were talking and laughing merrily. Not a care in the world did they seem to have.

There was a young girl among them, who happened to glance at the window of a jewellery store which they passed. On display there was a beautiful, brilliant diamond bracelet. How it sparkled and shone! The girl's eyes opened wide. She went close to the window to inspect the price. It was far too high – she could not afford it.

She caught up with her friends – but she was not the happy, laughing, bubbly girl that she had been five minutes earlier. Her cheerful, buoyant attitude had been replaced by a mood of glum disappointment.

This is the worst part about wanting things – getting them may give you momentary happiness. But not being able to get them often makes you miserable!

Practical Suggestion No. 7
Develop A Healthy Sense Of Humour

Humour is perhaps the best antidote to stress.

When you laugh out loud, you will find your body, mind and heart relaxing!

Laugh a lot. Laughter is a stress reducer. Try to be with people who bring laughter into your lives.

Learn to laugh at yourself – and you will find that stress and tension melt away.

There was a little girl who could not pronounce the word "Spaghetti." The more she tried, the funnier became her pronunciation.

"P-ppassghetti…" she would stammer. "Saphetti…" and she would end up in tears everytime. Her father advised her, "Don't take it so seriously, honey! If you can't pronounce a word – so what? Just laugh it off!"

This proved to be an excellent therapy. Next time she could not say "Spaghetti" she laughed out aloud. She was amazed when the others around her began to laugh with her. They were not laughing at her – in fact, everyone was having such fun!

As the girl grew older, she learnt to pronounce "Spaghetti" correctly. But every time she uttered the word right, she would think of the great fun she had with pasghetti and gaspetti!

People today, have forgotten to laugh. They have stopped smiling. What a sad loss this is!

A woman once said to me, "I have been married for twelve months – and during this period, my husband has smiled at me only three times." Just imagine – three smiles in one long year!

Laughter is an all-round tonic. It is a physical tonic; it is a mental tonic; it is a spiritual tonic.

Laughter strengthens the lungs. Laughter aids circulation. Laughter helps digestion. Laughter strengthens the immune system. But you must laugh *with* others – and not laugh *at* others.

During the course of a speech, Pandit Jawaharlal Nehru remarked, "Some of the happiest moments of my life were spent on the lap of a woman – who was not my wife."

The audience were shocked. What was Nehru saying? Did he mean what he said?

With a broad smile, Nehru added, "That woman was the wife of my father!"

At a meeting that Nehru was to address, a young man was asked to greet him. When he faced the microphone, the young man became nervous. Panic-struck, he stammered, "Ladies and gentlemen, Shakespeare has said… Shakespeare has said… Shakespeare…" He was so tense that he could not carry on.

Pandit Nehru eased the tense situation with his lovely sense of humour. He got up, took the mike from the boy and told him, "Young man, Shakespeare has said that you must hand the mike over to me!"

The famous writer, Mark Twain, approached his neighbour to borrow a book which he wanted to read. The neighbour said to him coldly, "You can read the book if you like, right here in my house. I can't allow you to take it away!"

A few days later, the neighbour came to Mark Twain and asked, "Can I borrow your lawn mower?" Mark Twain replied, "You can certainly borrow my lawn mower – but use it right here. I can't allow you to take it away from my house!"

Bishop Fulton Sheen had to deliver a lecture in an unfamiliar city. He arrived very early at the Hotel where he was to stay. So he decided that he would walk to the venue of the meeting, rather than take a cab. He took directions from the Hotel Manager and set out.

Before long, he realized that he had lost his way. He found a group of boys playing by the roadside. He approached them and asked, "Will one of you please guide me to the Town Hall?"

A smart boy happily volunteered to show him the way. As they walked, the boy asked him, "What brings you to our city, Sir?"

"I am to deliver a lecture at the Town Hall this evening," answered the Bishop.

"Oh!" said the boy impressed. "What is the topic of the lecture?"

"The Way to Heaven," answered the Bishop.

The boy burst out laughing. He laughed till tears ran down his cheeks.

"What makes you laugh?" asked the Bishop. "Do you think the way to Heaven is a laughing matter?"

"No, no," said the boy, "It's so funny. You don't know the way to the Town Hall – and you are going to deliver a lecture on the way to Heaven!"

There was a blind man. He would stand at a street corner, and hold out his hand. People would drop coins or notes into his hands.

There was a man who drove past the corner in his car, everyday. He would halt at the corner, stop his car, get out and hand a five rupee note to the blind man.

This went on successively for many days. One fine day, when he heard the car coming to a halt and the door opening and shutting, he held out both his hands, expectantly.

The kind donor was surprised to see two hands outstretched. "What is this Baba," he said, "Why are you stretching both your hands today?"

"Kind sir," replied the man. "Business is so good these days that I have opened a branch."

The rich man was so delighted with his reply that he placed a 500-rupee note in the new "branch."

Adam asked God, "Why did you make Eve so beautiful?"

"So that you may be able to love her," God replied.

"And why did you make her so stupid?" snapped Adam.

"So that she may be able to love you," God smiled and answered.

Yes – laugh and laugh a lot. Laughter is a stress reducer, a stress buster. Develop a humorous attitude and you will be free from stress.

Practical Suggestion No 8
Develop Faith, Cultivate Faith

Faith is not blind. Faith is seeing with the eyes of the mind. Even as we have two physical eyes with which we are able to see the wonderful things that are around us – trees, flowers, stars, streams, hills and dales, forests and mountains, even so with the eyes of faith we can perceive goodness, peace and calm all around us.

God loves each and every one of us and He has a plan for us. He will provide for all our needs. St. Teresa wanted to build an orphanage. She had only three shillings. But she was not tensed or worried about it. She said to those who ridiculed her: "With three shillings, Teresa can do nothing. But with God and three shillings there is nothing that Teresa cannot do."

If fear knocks on the door of your heart, send faith to open it and you will be free from distress.

Two men were ship wrecked. They landed on an island which was uninhabited. Out of the branches of trees, they built a cottage for themselves. One of them was a man of faith. But the other was an unbeliever, a sceptic. Everyday, the man of faith would affirm to himself: "There is a meaning of mercy in everything that happens. God will never forsake us: He will surely rescue us." But the unbeliever kept on fuming and fretting. "There is no God!" he would exclaim. Everyday, both of them would go and stand on the shore and wave their hands and handkerchiefs in the hope that some distant steamer would sight them and rescue them. The days passed by. One day as the two of them returned to their cottage, they found that the cottage had caught fire.

"Don't be depressed," pleaded the believer. "Friend, there must be a meaning in this, too. Trust in Him! He will never forsake us." Exasperated, the skeptic shouted: "You and your

God – I have nothing to do with the two of you."

The next morning, as they went to the shore, they saw a small boat approaching. They were surprised.

"We saw the flames leaping," the captain of the boat explained. "We felt surely there must be someone who needed help."

Once again the believer exclaimed: "There is a meaning of mercy in everything that happens. Blessed be His Name!"

Miracles do happen – in the lives of individuals who lay their trust in God!

Sometime ago, I read concerning a woman. She lost her husband who left her very little money. Soon after her husband's death, she received a bill for a large amount which she remembered having already paid. She could not locate the receipt. The bill collection department called her and finally warned her that if she did not pay the amount, she would be dragged to a court of law. The widow had faith in the Lord. She was not tensed. She was sure the Lord would take care of her.

The next day, a butterfly entered her house. Her small son fell in love with it and started chasing it. The butterfly flew behind her sofa set. The little boy insisted that the sofa be shifted so that he could play with the butterfly. The mother with great difficulty, shifted the sofa, and to her surprise found the receipt she was frantically searching for.

"How gracious Thou art, O Lord!" she exclaimed.

Faith is the light that always lights your path, no matter how dark the world may be around you.

A mother and her child were alone at home one night. When they were about to get into bed, the mother switched off the light and the room was dark. A sudden fear gripped the child. The woman opened the window, and up in the sky, the moon shone bright.

"Mother, is the moon God's light?" asked the child.

"Yes dear," replied the mother.

"Will God switch off His light when He goes to sleep?" asked the child anxiously.

"No, my dear," said the mother. "God never goes to sleep, and His light is never switched off."

"Well then," smiled the child. "As long as God is awake, I'm not afraid!"

This is the reassurance that we can all have – our Father is always awake. Why should we give in to stress when His light shines upon us?

On the pathways of life we face different types of weather – stormy and smooth, wild and mild. We have to face difficulties and dangers, diseases and death. We feel frightened. If only we cultivate the faith that such experiences come to us, not without a purpose – we will never be stressful.

The cure for stress is trust. We lay our trust on banks which fail, on bonds whose values fluctuate, on friends who betray us, on earthly power and dominion, on worldly goods which are perishable. We try to build our security on the things that are themselves insecure. As a result our lives become a ceaseless struggle. Struggle means uncertainty. Struggle means worry and anxiety, struggle means stress and tension. Much of our time is spent in providing for some untoward happening, which may not occur at all. We spend our time on making our living – and we are left with no time to enjoy the benefit thereof!

If only we learn to believe in God, trust in Him completely – cooperate with His Will – we would be supremely happy.

Therefore try to greet difficulties with a smile. Never forget that God is in charge of the Universe. He is protecting you, guiding you, guarding you. He will never fail you – then no fear will touch you.

A botanist who was collecting samples from a hill slope came across some rare species of flowers, which were located in a narrow ravine, just beneath a steep precipice. He was very anxious to collect a few specimens. But how could he reach the flowers?

He thought for a while. Then he called his eight-year old son, who was out for the day with him. He tied a rope around the boy's waist. He explained to the little boy what he had to do – which samples he had to collect. Then he gently lowered the boy down the edge of the cliff.

When the boy was drawn up after having successfully accomplished his errand, someone asked him, "Tell me, little one. Weren't you afraid?"

"No, of course not!" answered the boy. "My father was holding the rope!"

If only we could develop such faith - we could sail smoothly even during the stormiest weather!

Practical Suggestion No. 9

Take Care Of Your Breathing

You can overcome stress by changing your breathing pattern. You must learn how to breathe in the right way. Our breathing is rapid and shallow. On an average we breathe in and out 16 breaths in a minute. Our breathing is chest breathing. If you keep your hand on the chest while you are breathing, you will notice that your chest moves while you breathe. Chest breathing is stressful breathing. It is like parking your car, but leaving the engine on. Such things really do happen. A man was in a very stressful state. He parked his car, but left the engine on. The machine kept on working, running until it stopped. Similarly with chest breathing our bodies become stressful. What we need to practise is belly breathing. When we are born we are belly breathers. Look at a new born babe, watch its breathing, you will notice that when it breathes in and breathes out, its belly also responds similarly.

Initially, you need to practice awareness. Atleast for 10 times every few hours practise belly breathing. The more you practice belly breathing, the more peaceful and calm you will be and tension will not touch your body and mind.

Practical Suggestion No. 10
You Must Practise The Technique Of Relaxation

You must relax at least twice everyday. You must relax your body, relax your limbs, relax your muscles. There are several methods, several techniques to help you achieve relaxation of body and mind. You can pick up any one which suits you – but you must make sure you practise it regularly!

I have my own simple method of relaxation. Everytime I sit down to meditate, everytime I enter into the depths of silence within, I relax completely.

Any teacher of yoga will teach you to practise the *shavasana* – the dead man's posture. This is a very easy technique which we can all follow.

The important thing to remember is that in this process of relaxation, it is not the body which must relax – not merely every muscle, every limb and every nerve of the body – but also the mind, the thoughts, the emotions, the heart and its feelings which must be relaxed completely.

Remember one thing when you practise relaxation – the one life flows through all of us. Not merely through human beings, but through all creatures, through every thing that is. The one life flows through me, through every one of you, flows through every branch of every tree – flows indeed through the very air you breathe. Relax in the thought of this inter-relatedness of life.

I think of the body as built up of five *tatwas* – five essences – earth, air, fire, water, ether. And the Universe, this wide, vast, wonderful Universe is also built up of the same five elements. What then is this body, in the context of this vast Universe? This body is a drop of water in this huge expanse, the vast ocean that is the Universe. It is but a drop, bobbing up and down on the surface of the ocean of the Universe – a drop of water which is buoyed up, sustained, upheld by the wide expanse of water. In such a condition, the little drop of water must learn to abandon itself to the ocean – and as it abandons itself, it enters into a wonderful state of relaxation!

Your method of relaxation must be simple and natural. When I relax, I feel like a child in the arms of my Mother, in the safe, everlasting arms of the Mother Divine. I feel that I am at the Lotus Feet of the Lord, gently touching His ankles. When you are in such a state of complete relaxation, you lay yourself open to the great power of God. The great power of God flows in and through you – and it can work wonders for you!

Most of the time we are tensed without realizing it. Even when we go to sleep, our body and mind are not relaxed: we carry the tensions of the day with us and so do not have restful sleep. What is needed is to relax – if possible, twice every day.

There are many methods of relaxation; each person must follow the one that best suits him or her. Here is a simple, easy eleven-step method:

1. Lie on your back on the floor (or a carpet). Or sit on the floor in a comfortable posture. Or in a chair with your feet gently touching the floor. Take a few deep breaths, exhaling each slowly, completely emptying the lungs.

2. Imagine yourself in the loving, immediate and personal presence of the Lord (your Beloved). You are sitting at His Lotus Feet with your arms girdling His ankles, your head resting on His feet. Say to yourself, "Here is true rest. Here is true relaxation. In Thy presence, fears and frustrations, worries and anxieties, depressions and disappointments, tensions and tribulations

vanish as mist before the rising sun. I am relaxed. Relax... relax... relax."

3. To relax a muscle, you must first tighten it, then let it go. As you let it go, it may, perhaps, help you to utter the words, "Let go, let go, let God!"

4. Turn your attention to the muscles around the eyes. Relax-relax-relax. Open the eyes and imagine that the eyelids have become heavy. Let them drop on the eyes. Lift them and let them shut three times.

5. Move on to the muscles around the mouth. Tighten them and let go. Relax-relax-relax.

6. Relax your facial muscles. Clench your teeth, then relax, letting your face go limp. Relax-relax-relax.

7. Repeat the process throughout the body: neck, right shoulder, elbow, forearm, wrist, hand, fingers, left shoulder, elbow, forearm, wrist, hand, fingers, back, chest, abdomen,

buttocks, calves, ankles, feet, toes. Push your toes down toward the carpet, stretch and relax. Pull your feet up toward the legs, stretch and relax. Relax-relax-relax.

8. Breathe in and stretch your whole body, relax and exhale. Repeat this three times. Relax-relax-relax. You are calm, relaxed, peaceful, serene. You are resting at the Lotus Feet of the Lord-calm, relaxed, peaceful, serene.

9. You are now lighter than air, moving upwards, upwards, floating as a cloud – calm, relaxed, peaceful, serene.

10. You are in the presence of the Lord. Offer this simple prayer: "Thou art by me, a living and radiant Presence, and I am relaxed, calm, peaceful, serene." Repeat the prayer a few times. You are now completely relaxed.

11. When you wish to close this exercise in relaxation, rub the palms of your hands together, place them gently on the eyelids, and gently open the eyes.

Our lives need to be renewed, if possible, daily – through contact with God. The rain of God's mercy pours every day; and those of us who receive it are washed clean, renewed and re-strengthened for the struggle of life, as servants of God. May I suggest to you a simple exercise? Every morning, as you sit in silence, close your eyes and imagine the Life of God coursing through every part of your body filling it through and through. The Life of God is in us already: we have to be conscious of it. Say to yourself: Every moment the Life of God – call Him what Name you will, Krishna, Buddha, Christ, Guru Nanak: They are all so many names of Him who is Nameless – is filling every nerve and cell and fibre of my being!

Then begin with the head. Feel the Life of God coursing through your head, and say, "The Life of God is renewing, revitalizing my entire brain, every nerve and nerve centre, and the entire cerebro-spinal system. And my brain thinks the thoughts of God. It thinks in obedience to the Moral Law....

"The Life of God is renewing the entire sensory system. It is revitalizing the eyes; and now my eyes see more clearly, more purely. God's Light shines in and through them: and the Light of God is the Light of purity...

"God's Life is revitalizing my ears. They hear more clearly and they hear words that are good and noble; and they hear the music of God that thrills the universe from end to end....

"God's Life is revitalizing my nose.... God's Life is revitalizing my throat. How sweetly it sings the Name of God and the songs of saints of God! And it utters words that are sweet and true and helpful to humanity!"

Now pause for a moment. Then take in a deep breath and turn your attention to the lungs and the heart. Imagine the Life of God renewing, revitalizing, the chest and the heart. The heart is the seat of emotions, and because God's Life is in it, I shall be emotionally balanced, calm and serene in every situation and circumstance of life.

Turn your attention to your arms and hands. They are the hands of God. They are instruments of God's help and healing in this world of suffering and pain....Think of the stomach and other organs...Then come to your legs, knees, and feet. The feet are now firmly set on the path of righteousness and self-realization.

After covering your entire body, concentrate once again on the heart. The heart is the Sanctuary of the Temple, the Abode of the Lord. And now imagine the Lord seated in the heart – for that is where He is already – His Love, His Wisdom, His Strength, His Intelligence, His Joy, His Peace, all centred there and reaching out to every part of your body and outside to your dear and near ones, and to your friends and "foes" alike.

It will take you longer to read this than to put this simple exercise into practice. Repeat this exercise, as often as you can, during the day. But do it at least twice everyday – in the morning and at night. And you will soon, very soon, see the effects of it. Your health will improve. Your mind will be more relaxed and alert. Your heart will be more responsive to the pain of others. And you will grow into a fuller, richer, deeper consciousness of the presence of God. He will be more real to you than the things of this earth. New love and longing for Him will wake up within your heart. And you will aspire to dedicate all you are, and all you have, at His Lotus Feet for the service of suffering creation. You will live and move and have your being in the Joy and Peace of God. You will be blessed among the children of men.

Practical Suggestion No. 11
Practise Silence Everyday

We live in a noisy world, a noisome world. All the noises around us create stress. Even as particles of dust cling to our clothes, even so particles of noise cling to our minds, our hearts, nay, our very souls.

When our clothes are soiled, we wash them with soap and water. How do we clean our souls, which are polluted by the noise around us? We must wash them in the waters of silence – the flowing river of silence. We need to take dips in this river again and again.

Dr. Deborah Bright is regarded as an authority on stress; and her recommendation to overcome stress is what she calls PQT. PQT is Personal Quiet Time. Dr. Bright recommends two sessions of PQT – 20 minutes in the morning,

20 minutes in the evening - everday. If you have these two sessions regularly, tension and stress cannot touch you.

A philosopher once asked a king, "Who do you think is the happiest being in the world?"

"God," replied the king, and he added, "The happiest of men is he who is closest to God."

"How may we get close to God?" he was asked.

"Through the practice of silence!" he was asked.

Significant are the words of the *Upanishad:* "The mind alone is the cause of man's bondage; the mind is also, the instrument of man's liberation."

It is silence which can still the mind, so that the mind is calm and clear as the surface of the lake on a windless day. In silence, the mind will become a source of indescribable joy and peace - and tension and stress will vanish, as dew before the rising sun.

To sit in silence, you must learn to be still. "The more a man does," says an English mystic, "the more he is and exists. And the more he is and exists, the less of God is and exists within him."

Let me sit in silence, so that the God within me awakens. Let me sit still, as a silent spectator viewing the shifting scenes of a fickle mind. Let me but sit, as I sat long ago, in a theatre watching a play. The actors appeared on the stage, played their respective roles and disappeared. I kept looking on! So too, let me keep looking at the thoughts that come and go – rushing out of the unknown depths of my mind. They are not mine. I have nothing to do with them. They come: let them come. They will soon pass out, leaving the chamber of my mind calmer, cleaner and brighter.

Sitting in silence, you can pray. You can meditate upon the Lord. You can engage yourself in a loving and intimate conversation with God. God is not from you afar. He is wherever we are. He is here. He is now. Anchor your hopes and aspirations in His safe harbour. Where He is – there is absolute Peace.

Practical Suggestion No. 12
Help Others

Because it is only in the measure in which you help others, that you forget your problems, your own emperic ego. In the measure you forget your lower self, you get into contact with the higher self. And when you get into contact with the higher self, you become masters of stress.

There is no stress-buster stronger than this – go out of yourself and help others. Forget your petty self, your empirical self. It is this petty self that is the home of tension.

A young man met me several years ago; he was a bundle of tension. He was in jitters. He had been rejected by a girl he loved. He said he was on his way to the railway station to throw himself under a running train.

But the thought occurred to him to see me before he ended his life.

I placed my hand on his shoulders and said to him, "Yes, why not – but just before going to the railway station, do something for me."

"Why not?" he said, "I shall do anything for you."

I passed on to him a ten-rupee note and said to him, "Go to the fruit market and purchase a little fruit. Then go to the government hospital, to the poor patients' ward and distribute the fruits. Then come and meet me."

The man returned to me after two hours. He was a changed man. "I never knew there was so much suffering in the world," he exclaimed. "My sorrow is nothing compared to the pain of these little children – who inspite of their illnesses, continue to smile. I shall not end my life. From today, I shall dedicate my life to the service of the suffering ones!"

Kindness is the balm that softens and smooths the rough patches of life. It is the healing touch that can take away the pain and misery of human existence. And when you send out kindness to others, you will find it returns to you manifold.

The famous English poet, Wordsworth, relates an incident from his early life which left a lasting impression on him. As he was wandering through a wood, he came across a weak, old man who was trying desperately to cut at the root of a tree. The task was so far beyond his feeble strength, that he was near collapse. The poet, a young man, seized his axe and at one blow, severed the tangled root. The old man's gratitude was like an avalanche, the poet recalled in memorable lines:

> *The tears into his eyes were brought,*
> *And thanks and praises seemed to run*
> *So fast out of his heart, I thought*
> *He never would be done.*

Such is the power of a single act of kindness!

A few men were requested to meet Lord Shaftesbury at the Railway Station. "How shall we know his Lordship?" they enquired.

The answer they received was significant: "You will see a tall man getting out of the train. *He will be helping somebody or the other.* That will be Lord Shaftesbury."

Indeed, kindness is the true mark of a great man.

Kindness is the greatest antidote to stress. Doing something for someone else dissolves your stress and tension. Everyone of us can practise a little kindness – it does not have to be a great act of service. Write a letter to a friend; make a phone-call; visit a lonely neighbour; smile at the people you meet. You will find that these little acts of kindness flood your own life with sunshine – and where there is the sunshine of kindness, stress and tension cannot exist! As my Beloved Master, Sadhu Vaswani, has said, "If you wish to be happy, make others happy!"

In your happy moments -
> glorify God!

In your difficult moments -
> pray to God!

In your quiet moments -
> spend time with God!
In your painful moments -
> praise God!
Every moment -
> draw close to God!

I met a centenarian. He was very joyful, happy and active. I asked him the secret of his peace. He said: Think positively, eat sparingly, exercise regularly, walk as much as you can and see that your thoughts and actions are always clean. There should be no feeling of guilt in your mind.

To this I would add, practise silence for 15 minutes everyday and extend your hand of helpfulness to as many as you can.

Stress Busters
(One for every day of the month)

- Always remember that God is in charge of the Universe.

  He is the controller of individuals and nations.

  And nothing can ever go wrong!

- Life is full of joy to the man who thinks positively and speaks positively.

- See that your face always wears a smile: smiles and tension can never go together.

  Whenever you feel tension mounting up, just smile: you will break the force of tension.

- All burden is borne by the Lord. Not merely the burden of our individual lives, not merely the burden of the nations, not merely the burden of the earth or the solar system, but the burden of all universes, the galaxies and the nebulae, huge stellar systems in the making – the entire burden is ultimately borne by the Lord.

How foolish of us, then, to be carrying our little burdens on our weak shoulders!

- Hurry is the number one cause of tension.

  Slow down your pace!

- Faith is seeing with the eyes of the heart.

  The man of faith, therefore, rejoices in everything as it comes to him and moves on – ever onward, forward, Godward!

- Never carry the tension of one moment to another.

  Has some one harmed me? Has someone spread scandals against me? Has some one behaved rudely towards me?

  Let me forget it all, thinking of the unity of all life.

- This is the secret of the truly stress-free man – he walks with God today and trusts Him for tomorrow!

- In this transitory world, only the present moment belongs to you.

  The moment that is just over is no longer yours. The moment to come may not belong to you at all.

  The present moment is best utilised not in worrying over what may have happened or what is yet to happen, but in praising God for the joy of living with Him.

- The man who has faith in God is released from the bondage of fear – for fear is a child of unfaith and is a constant source of stress.

- Never get upset, irritated, excited.

  Never lose your temper.

  Peace of mind is your richest treasure.

  Let nothing, no one take it away from you!

- In all conditions of life, let us thank the Lord! Let us make it a habit – to praise the Lord at every step, in every round of life! In the midst of fear and frustration, worry and anxiety, depression and disappointment, let these words come out of the very depths of your heart - "Thank you, God! Thank you God!"

- In every situation, do the very best you can and leave the result to the Lord.

- God is our Friend – the Friend of all friends, the one Constant, Unchanging Friend. He is available to us all 24 hrs of the day and night. He is ever ready to help us. How many of us seek His help?

- Prayer is the great bulwark against worry. How often do we not lay waste our powers in worry over things which have happened to us or which may happen in the coming days! Every worry means a strain on the nerves. The more we worry, the more tense we become, robbing from us our own rest and peace of mind and heart. Instead of worrying let us learn to turn to God in prayer and trust!

- Nothing is wrong with the world: the wrong that I see is due to my defective sight. I do not have to pray for the world to be changed. I have to pray that I may be cured of my defective eye-sight to be able to see that all is and has always been well with the world.

- Let me do nothing that may disturb my peace of mind and heart. Let my daily life be so regulated as to strengthen the inner calm, not take away from it. So let me avoid over work. And let me not be in a hurry to do anything. Let me go about my work quietly, gently and lovingly – my mind and heart devoted to the Lotus Feet of the Lord.

- There is no security in physical or material things. True security belongs to him who has developed a child like trust in God. He is the source of all that a man needs – property, power, peace, strength, wisdom, health, happiness and harmony.

- Take care to see that your tension does not accumulate. Therefore practise relaxing every day and learn to take your troubles to God.

- The foundation of a healthy body is a happy mind. Therefore, let nothing agitate you or disturb your inner peace.

- We feel upset because we are attached. One way to face an upsetting situation is to say, as Sadhu Vaswani used to say: "God upsets our plans to set up his own and his plans are always perfect."

- There is truly one way of achieving peace of mind. And that is the way of self-relization. Once your realize yourself there is no more stress, no more tension. Your abide in a state of tranquility and peace.

- Why is it that we lose our peace of mind? Because our wishes, our desires are crossed. And above our wishes is the Will of God. Accept His Will – you will never lose your peace.

- The secret of relaxation is in two words: "Let Go!" The more we let go, the more do we conserve our energy for the constructive and creative tasks of life.

- Overcome stress by understanding what STRESS stands for

   S-Smile. Keep on smiling.

   T-Tolerance. Grow in tolerance.

   R-Relax. Never become tense.

   E-Easy. Take it easy, but be not lazy.

   S-Service. Keep serving.

   S-Silence. Practise silence and thereby turn to God.

- Let us not offer resistance to Life. Resistance inevitably leads to wastage of energy which could be used for constructive ends. Acceptance is not passive. To accept is to triumph over circumstances and not let them touch the joy and peace of the soul.

- So many of our ills would be cured, if only we could change the pattern of our mind. Change the mind and you will change the world!

- The Bhagavad Gita tells us, "Man is his own friend: man is his own foe!" We are our own friends and we are our own enemies. No one outside of us can do us any harm. If we would be our own friends, let us adopt a positive attitude towards life.

- Take care of your thoughts – as you think, so you become. Fill your mind with happy thoughts. Unclutter your mind of lust, hatred, greed, selfishness, miserliness, envy, jealousy, ill-will, resentment. Only then can you hope to be happy!

- It is not what happens to us that really matters, it is the way we react to what happens. And if we react to what happens to us in the right way, we become masters of stress and we become creators of valuable driving energy.

- Every time that I feel irritated, every time that I feel annoyed, I may not show it, but I am spending so much of my emotional energy in vain. Refuse to be an emotional spendthrift!

Dada J.P. Vaswani needs no introduction to readers of inspirational literature. He is regarded as one of the leading spiritual luminaries of India, a practical philosopher and man of God whose grace has reached and influenced thousands of people all over the world.

A gifted writer and brilliant orator, Dada J.P. Vaswani has been the recipient of several honours, including the prestigious U Thant Peace Award. He has written over 80 books which have been translated into several Indian and foreign languages.